MOUNTAIN TASTING

Yama areba yama o miru
ame no hi ame o kiku
haru natsu aki fuyu
ashita mo yoroshi
yūbe mo yoroshi

If there are mountains, I look at the mountains;
On rainy days I listen to the rain.
Spring, summer, autumn, winter.
Tomorrow too will be good.
Tonight too is good.

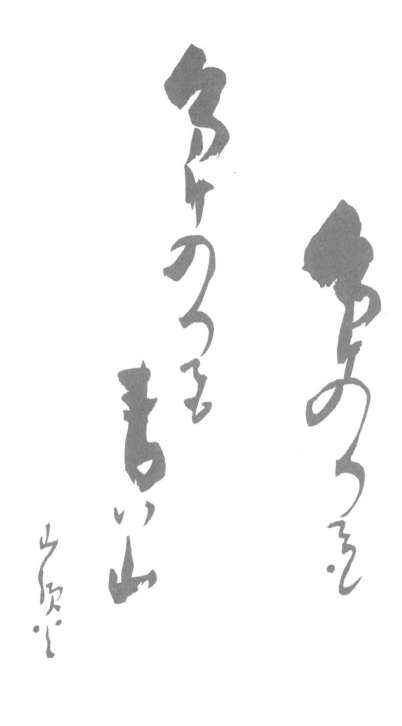

MOUNTAIN TASTING

Zen Haiku by Santōka Taneda

Translated and introduced by John Stevens

WEATHERHILL
New York & Tokyo

A NOTE ON THE FRONTISPIECE. One
of Santōka's best-known haiku (see no.
18, p. 37), in his own calligraphy.

First edition, 1980
Fourth printing, 1991

Published by Weatherhill, Inc., New York, with editorial offices
at Tanko-Weatherhill, Inc., 8-3 Nibancho, Chiyoda-ku, Tokyo
102, Japan. Protected by copyright under terms of the Inter-
national Copyright Union; all rights reserved. Printed and first
published in Japan.

LIBRARY OF CONGRESS CATALOGING IN PUBLICATION DATA:
Taneda, Santōka, 1882–1940. / Mountain tasting. / Bibliography:
p. / I. Title. / PL817.A62A28 / 895.6'14 / 80-97 / ISBN 0-8348-
0151-5

FOR MY PARENTS
ARTHUR AND ANNE STEVENS
WITH GRATITUDE

CONTENTS

INTRODUCTION

Recently, a remarkable interest in the life and poetry of the mendicant Zen priest Santōka Taneda (1882–1940) has developed in Japan. Collections of Santōka's haiku and accounts of his life are being published regularly. At present, more books on Santōka are available than perhaps on any other Japanese poet, ancient or modern. In addition, he is considered to be a great Zen master much like Ikkyū, Hakuin, and Ryōkan. How is it that such an eccentric, drink-loving haiku poet came to be so highly regarded?

From a literary standpoint, Santōka's poems are generally admired for their unadorned style, representative of the "new haiku movement," but this does not explain his great popularity with all types of people, not only poets and scholars. Whatever the literary merit of his work, far more important are the special Zen qualities of simplicity (*wabi*), solitude (*sabi*), and impermanence (*mujō*) conveyed in a modern setting by his haiku. Poetry has often been nothing more than a pastime for many in China and Japan, so that portrayals of "poverty," "solitude," "meditation," and so on were mere conventions. In Santōka's case, however, such themes were absolute; no one was poorer, more alone, or more anguished. Hence his poems are alive, cutting to the marrow of existence. There is no dichotomy between poetry and poet, life and emotion.

Santōka's life embodies the Zen spirit in three ways. First, since his life and poetry were one, he represents the ideal of "no duplicity." In any art or discipline it is essential to unify thought, speech, and action. Second, he did not mimic anyone else. This is rare in any society. In Japan, the life of a wandering poet is considered the most impermanent, irregular, and individualistic of all occupations. It is a life of freedom from everything: material possessions, mental concepts, social norms. Third is Santōka's simplicity of expression. In his verses there is nothing extra, no pretense, no artificiality. They can be understood at once without analysis. Sharp and direct, Santōka's haiku epitomize Zen writing: pure experience, free of intellectual coloring.

Santōka's appeal is not limited to Japan. Haiku and Zen practice are established throughout the world. As a man of the twentieth century, Santōka is close to us in thought and temperament. Fortunately, his haiku lose little in translation, so with the publication of this collection of his poems, people of all countries will now be able to share in his unique "journey into the depths of the human heart."

SANTŌKA'S LIFE   Shōichi Taneda—now better known as Santōka—was born in the village of Sabare in the Hōfu district of Yamaguchi Prefecture on December 3, 1882. His father, a large and impressive figure, was a landowner and active in local politics but not very good at running his business or personal affairs. Shōichi was the second child, first boy, and one more sister and two more brothers were born in the next few years.

Shōichi was good at his studies and displayed an interest in literature as early as elementary school. Unfortunately, his father was a dissolute womanizer who carried on with several mistresses at a time. When he wasn't playing with the ladies he was politicking, so he was rarely home. While he was vacationing in the mountains with one of his mistresses, his wife committed suicide by throwing herself into a well on the family property. She was thirty-three years old. Shōichi, just eleven at the time, never completely recovered from the shock of seeing his mother's lifeless body being lifted from the well, and this tragic event affected him throughout his life. Afterwards he was raised by his grandmother.

In 1896 he entered middle school and began to write traditional-style haiku. In 1902 he enrolled in the literature department of Waseda University in Tokyo. There, following the custom, he took a pen name; from then on he called himself Santōka ("Burning Mountain Peak"). He began to drink heavily, suffered a nervous breakdown, and was unable to complete the first-year requirements. In addition, his father was in financial straits and could no longer afford the tuition, so Santōka had to return home.

Santōka arrived in his home town in July 1904 at the beginning of the Russo-Japanese War. His father sold off some of the family land and purchased a sakè brewery that he opened with Santōka in 1907. Two years later, at the insistence of his father, who thought a wife might help cut down Santōka's drinking, an arranged marriage took place with Sakino Satō, a pretty girl from a neighboring village. However, the union was troubled right from the beginning, and Santōka never adjusted to married life. The following year their only child, Ken, was born.

In 1911 Santōka came under the influence of Seisensui Ogiwara (1884–1976), the founder of the *jiyūritsu*, or free-style, school of haiku. Following the death of Shiki (1867–1903), who had revitalized and revolutionized the world of haiku, there were two main streams in the haiku world: one working in a more or less traditional form using modern themes, and the other, the *shinkeikō*, or new-development, movement, which abandoned the standard 5–7–5 syllable pattern and the obligatory use of a word to indicate the season, or *kigo*. In April 1911 Seisensui established the magazine *Sōun* to expound the theory that it is necessary for a poet to express what is in his heart in his own language without regard to any fixed form. Seisensui felt that haiku should be an impression of one's inner experiences; individual symbolism is most important. Seisensui stressed *jiyū* (freedom), *jiko* (self), and *shizen* (nature), together with the elements of *chikara* (strength) and *hikari* (brightness), for his new haiku. Seisensui was influenced by European literature, especially Goethe and Schiller, and his poetry was essentially a combination of Japanese sensitivity and Western expressionism. However, it was neither agnostic nor scientific like much of the other new haiku. Haiku is a "way" rather than mere literature or art. Such a highly individualistic and subjective theory was criticized by many traditionalists, but it greatly appealed to Santōka. Beginning in 1913, Santōka became one of the main contributors to *Sōun* and the free-style school.

Seven of Santōka's verses were printed in 1913, and the following year Santōka met Seisensui for the first time at a poetry meeting. Santōka was active composing poetry and essays for the next few years and became an editor of *Sōun* in 1916. In the meantime, however, the sakè brewery was turning into a disaster. The father continued to run around with women, and the son kept drinking up what little profit they occasionally made. More and more family property was sold off to prop up the brewery. In 1915 the entire stock spoiled, and in April the next year the brewery went bankrupt and the Taneda family lost everything. The father fled one night with one of his mistresses, while Santōka and his family moved to Kumamoto City, where one of his friends offered to help him.

Santōka originally planned to open a secondhand bookstore, but that failed to work out, so his wife took over and started a store specializing in picture frames. Santōka continued his heavy drinking, and the marriage deteriorated. In 1918 his younger brother Jirō committed suicide (his other brother had died in infancy), another shock for the high-strung poet.

Santōka and his wife drifted apart, and in 1919 he decided to go to Tokyo to seek work. His first job was a part-time position with a cement firm. Later he found a temporary position as a clerk in the Hitotsubashi municipal library. Santōka and his wife were legally divorced in 1920. Sakino continued to operate the store and raise their son. The following year Santōka's father died. Santōka was offered a permanent position at the library and he accepted. Unfortunately, he proved no better at this job than at making sakè. He suffered another nervous breakdown and was forced to retire a year and a half after he began. On September 1, 1923, the Great Kantō Earthquake struck Tokyo and destroyed much of the city. Santōka escaped injury, but his boardinghouse was reduced to rubble. He decided to return to Kumamoto, where he helped his former wife with the store.

Near the end of December 1924, Santōka, drunk and apparently intent on committing suicide, stood in the middle of some railroad tracks facing an oncoming train. The train screeched to a halt just in time, and Santōka was pulled out of the way. He was taken to a nearby Zen temple called Hōon-ji. The head priest there, Gian Mochizuki Oshō, did not reprimand or question Santōka: he didn't even ask his name. The monk fed Santōka and told him he could stay at the temple as long as he wished.

Santōka had long been interested in Zen. He had attended several lectures of the famous Zen master Kōdō Sawaki Rōshi in Kumamoto and had spent most of his spare time at the library in Tokyo reading books on Buddhism. Under Gian's direction Santōka sat in Zen meditation, chanted sutras, and worked around the temple. In 1925, at the age of forty-two, Santōka was ordained a Zen priest under the name Kōho after a Chinese Zen priest also named Taneda (Chung-t'ien in Chinese pronunciation) who was famous for cultivating a small rice field to raise enough food to support himself. Gian explained that Kōho Taneda is one who plows and cultivates the field of his heart.

Santōka's ex-wife Sakino joined the Methodist Church and became an active member soon after Santōka entered the temple. She never remarried, and Santōka continued to visit her and help with the store from time to time for the rest of his life.

After Santōka was ordained, Gian arranged for him to stay at Mitori Kannon-dō, a small temple on the outskirts of Kumamoto. Santōka supported himself by begging in the neighborhood, occasionally making longer trips to visit his friends in nearby towns. After a year of living alone in the temple, Santōka decided to make a pilgrimage. His first intention was to train at Eihei-ji, the head temple of the Sōtō Zen school, but he apparently realized it would be difficult for him as a forty-three-year-old man to practice with a group of priests in their early twenties, most of whom were putting in the required time in order to someday inherit their family temples. Santōka's monastery turned out to be the back roads and mountain paths of the countryside.

In April 1926 he started out on his first pilgrimage. His only possessions were his black priest's robe, his begging bowl, and his *kasa,* a large woven straw hat worn by traveling monks to shield them from the sun and rain. For the next four years Santōka was on a continual journey throughout southern Honshu, Kyushu, and Shikoku. He prayed at innumerable shrines and temples, visited famous sites, met with his friends, and attended poetry meetings. After a lapse of almost five years his poems began to appear in *Sōun* again.

In December 1930 he returned to Kumamoto and rented a small room. With the help of some friends who were publishers, he put out three issues of a little magazine called *Sambaku,* named after his boardinghouse. Six months after moving into Sambakukyo he was taken into custody for public drunkenness. (This requires some effort, since Japanese are very tolerant of drunkards.) He stayed at the picture-frame shop for a few months and then began another series of trips. In 1932, his friends found a small cottage for him in the mountain village of Ogōri in Yamaguchi Prefecture. Santōka called it Gochū-an after a verse in the *Lotus Sutra.** The cottage was rather dilapidated yet spacious, with three rooms, a well, and a tiny field surrounded by many fruit trees. He posted this sign:

---

* This verse refers to one member of a large group telling the others to call on the name of Kanzeon Bosatsu, the goddess of compassion; then all will be saved from calamities.

To All Visitors

—If you bring your favorite sweet or sour food with you
—And dance and sing unreservedly with the gentleness
  of the spring wind and autumn streams
—Without putting on airs or being downhearted, all
  will share great happiness.

This year also marked the publication of his first collection of haiku, *Hachi no Ko* (The Begging Bowl), produced by a friend's small publishing house.

From 1932 to 1938 Santōka divided his time between Gochū-an and traveling. He made trips to Hiroshima, Kobe, Kyoto, and Nagoya. In 1934 he fell ill and returned to his hermitage, Gochū-an. Sick and penniless, he contemplated suicide for a time but abandoned the idea after regaining his health, and began an eight-month journey to northern Honshu, retracing much of the route taken by the famous haiku-poet Bashō (1644–94) as described in *Oku no Hosomichi* (Narrow Road to the Deep North). During this period he published more issues of his journal *Sambaku,* in addition to putting out four more collections of his poetry: *Sōmokutō* (Grass and Tree Stupa, 1933), *Sangyō Suigyō* (Flowing with Mountains and Rivers, 1935), *Zassō Fūkei* (Weedscapes, 1936), and *Kaki no Ha* (Persimmon Leaves, 1938).

When he was staying at Gochū-an, he often had visitors from all parts of the country. Occasionally poetry meetings were held there. However, in 1938 Gochū-an literally collapsed and Santōka moved to a small hut in Yuda Hot Springs about eight miles away. He remained there a few months, set out on another trip, returned briefly, and then was off again. In December 1939 he settled down in Matsuyama City, Ehime Prefecture, in a little cottage that he named Issō-an, One Blade of Grass Hut.

In 1940 an expanded version of *Sōmokutō* was published containing selections from his previous works, including a sixth collection entitled *Kōkan* (Isolation) and published in

15

1939. His seventh and final collection, *Karasu* (Crows), was brought out in 1940 a few months after *Sōmokutō*.

Early in October 1940 a poetry meeting was held at Issō-an. The members of the group gathered at Issō-an, but found Santōka quite intoxicated, so they moved to a nearby member's house. They looked in on Santōka before they left and found him sleeping soundly. Uneasy, the wife of one of his friends went to see Santōka the next morning and discovered that he had departed on his final journey during the early morning hours of October 11, 1940.

THE WANDERING BEGGAR Santōka is said to have walked more than twenty-eight thousand miles during his travels as a wandering monk. His initial trips, especially the first one to Shikoku to visit the eighty-eight shrines and temples associated with the Buddhist saint Kōbō Daishi (Kūkai; 774–835), were pilgrimages to pray for the repose of his mother's troubled spirit. Later on, however, many of his trips were made without any particular destination.

> *Sate dochira e ikō kaze ga fuku*
> Well, which way should I go?
> The wind blows.

Renouncing the world, drifting here and there, living close to nature, settling now and then in a hermitage, and dying alone is a type of spirituality especially appreciated by the Japanese. Many of their favorite poets, priests, and artists were wanderers—Saigyō, Ippen Shōnin, Bashō, Sesshū, Enkū, to name a few. A life of travel is an abandoning of all that seems permanent or stable; life is reduced to absolute essentials, in the present moment, free of ordinary restrictions or constraints.

Whenever Santōka attempted to settle down, he was unable to do so for more than a few months. He wrote: "Too much

16

contact with people brings conflict, hatred, and attachment. To rid myself of inner conflicts and hatred I must walk.''

> *Nigoreru mizu no nagaretsutsu sumu*
> As muddy water flows
> It becomes clear.

Walking through the mountains and along the seacoast accompanied by butterflies and dragonflies, he had a rhythm in his stride that made poetry writing easier—one breath, one step, one verse. In another sense, traveling is a continuous search for our real home, the *furusato* Santōka so often speaks of in his poems.

Santōka was seeking freedom: ''To do what I want, and not to do what I don't—this is why I entered such a life.'' Japan was gearing toward the tragedy of World War II, and the government demanded conformity from all its citizens. Santōka passively resisted by letting his body and mind wander freely.

Once a reporter was interviewing one of Santōka's poet friends when Santōka happened to arrive unannounced. The reporter told Santōka: ''If everyone lived like you, society would be in big trouble.'' Santōka smiled and said: ''I'm one of society's warts, it's true. A big black wart on the face is hideous, but a small one is no problem. Sometimes people even have affection for their little blemishes. Please think of me like that.''

Like Bashō, Santōka noted that ''when you travel you truly come to understand human beings, poetry, and nature.'' Santōka was more extreme than Bashō, completely giving himself to *mujō* (impermanence) and *sabi* (solitude). Santōka was a beggar-monk who always traveled alone, flowing with the clouds and water.

He would generally beg for about three hours every day. Stopping to chant in front of a house, more often than not he would be chased away and verbally, and sometimes physically, abused. Usually he had to visit from fifteen to twenty homes (as the depression deepened he had to make thirty or more stops) before he had received enough for a day. As soon as he had received just enough rice and money for one day's food and lodging, he would stop immediately and go to the cheapest inn he could find. He never provided for the next day. "How can you be a beggar if you have extra money?" he asked.

Santōka would gratefully accept whatever was placed in his bowl, regardless of the quantity or quality. "Begging with a heart full of gratitude and respect, I hope to find the world of unlimited life and light. My pilgrimage is into the depths of the human heart. Begging is mutual gratitude and charity, the basis of society." Once an old woman mistakenly put a five-sen coin, a fairly large amount in those days, in Santōka's bowl. Later, after leaving the village, Santōka discovered the error; he walked back to the village, found the old woman, and returned the coin.

However, Santōka's begging was rather different from that of Ryōkan Oshō (1758–1831), the famous beggar-monk-poet of Echigo, who frequently left his begging bowl by the side of the road while he tossed a ball with the village children, played marbles with the local geishas, or picked flowers. When someone mentioned this contrast to Santōka, he replied: "My passions are too deep to do such a thing. If I don't have a begging bowl, I can't live. Therefore, I never forget my bowl."

It is rather remarkable that Santōka never fell seriously ill during his begging trips. When he did get sick, he recovered in one of two ways. Once when he developed a high fever, he was forced to lie down on the ground. An old woman came over to him and said: "I'll give you an offering if you recite the *Shushōgi* (excerpts from the writings of Dōgen Zenji) and the *Kannon Sutra*." Santōka staggered to his feet and began chanting. Totally absorbed in the words, he forgot about the old woman, his sickness, and the offering. After finishing forty minutes later, he felt completely recovered from his fever.

Another time in freezing weather he drank a great deal of sakè to keep warm and suddenly became violently ill, suffering from liver trouble. He was taken to a hospital and placed on a strict regimen of bitter medicine and no sakè. Santōka did not care for that, so he escaped from the hospital, went to the nearest shop, drank two cups of sakè, ate some *yudōfu* (boiled soybean cake), and was restored.

On his trips Santōka rose at 4:30, bathed, chanted the morning service, ate a tiny breakfast, and started out on a begging trip. When he had received enough, he would either return to the inn or move on to the next place, depending on his mood. He might even stay as long as a month if he liked the area and if the food and lodging were cheap.

Santōka usually received about thirty-five sen from his begging. The charge for a room at an inn ranged from twenty-five to thirty-five sen. Anything extra went for sakè, small amounts of tobacco, or post cards to send to his friends. He often shared his meager take with other beggars. Santōka described one of his favorite places like this: "The food is very cheap here, the salvation of this old hobo. Raw fish is five sen a plate, tempura five sen, *yudōfu* two sen. Even a drunkard like me can become a Buddha in this very body for thirty sen." He described his greatest happiness as "one room, one person, one light, one desk, one bath, and one cup of sakè."

Every evening he recorded in his journal the name of the inn, the sights he had seen, the money received from begging, his expenses for that day, and then the haiku he had written, together with his reflections. His journal was his self-portrait. In his travels he "touched this and that and recorded the mind's changing impressions." He poured his life into his haiku and journals, writing down his most intimate thoughts and arguing with himself. Occasionally he felt too attached to his journals; then he would burn them or throw them away. (Similarly, before he left Gochū-an he burned the few possessions he had accumulated.)

19

In his last journals we find these two entries that sum up his life: "This is the path I must follow—there is no other road for me to walk on. It is a path containing both pleasure and pain. It is far off yet definite. It is very narrow and steep. However, it is also a white path [of purity], full of amazing and wonderful things. It is not a cold and lifeless way.

"I am nothing other than a beggar-monk. There is nothing you can say about me except that I am a foolish pilgrim who spent his entire life wandering, like the drifting water plants that float from shore to shore. It appears pitiful, but I find happiness in this destitute, quiet life. Water flows, clouds move, never stopping or settling down. When the wind blows, the leaves fall. Like the fish swimming or the birds flying, I walk and walk, going on and on."

The day before his death Santōka went to visit a friend and told him: "After the poetry meeting tomorrow I'll be starting out on a journey. I want to throw myself into nature one last time. I haven't got long to live, and I want to be like the sparrows or wild elephants who die alone quietly in the fields."

SAKÈ, ZEN, AND HAIKU

> Days I don't enjoy:
> Any day I don't walk.
> Any day I don't drink sakè.
> Any day I don't compose haiku.

Sakè, Zen, and haiku were the three main elements of Santōka's life; they were always present together, often interchangeable and sometimes indistinguishable.

Santōka's Zen was not the sitting Zen (zazen) of Dōgen or the kōan Zen of Rinzai. It was "walking Zen." Santōka was very much like the Chinese monks of old who practiced walking rather than sitting meditation, gaining realization through contact with nature on long pilgrimages from one mountain temple to another. Such monks were solitary figures, attached to no institution or master. Walking was their zazen:

> Without anger, without speaking,
> Without covetousness,
> Walk slowly, walk steadily!

while begging was the discipline of killing selfish desires:

> Pierce the poverty of the poorest man,
> Throw yourself into the most foolish foolishness.
> Rather than imitate anyone else
> Use the nature you were born with.

In his travels Santōka attempted to accept everything that came his way without clinging to ideas of self and others, true or false, good or bad, life or death. This was not easy. "Adherence to things material and spiritual prevents me from being as free as the wind or flowing water."

> *Sutekirenai nimotsu no omosa mae ushiro*
> Baggage I cannot throw off,
> So heavy front and back.

Although Gian was a priest of the Sōtō Zen school, which emphasizes zazen and careful attention to detail, he understood Santōka's character and did not try to direct him into any established routine or practice. He gave Santōka a copy of the *Mumonkan*, a collection of kōans from Chinese Zen masters, to study on his travels. As it turned out, Santōka did meet many people (including the old woman that made him chant sutras when he was ill) who confronted him with various questions about Buddhism. One such dialogue went:

> "Where is the Way?" a fellow traveler demanded.
> "Under your feet. Straight ahead.
> You are standing on it right now," Santōka replied.
> "Where is the mind?"

"Everyday mind is the Way. When tea
is offered, drink it; when rice is
served, eat it. Respect your parents
and look after your children. Mind is
not inside or outside."

Santōka made the following list, which might be entitled
"My Religion":

My Three Precepts:
Do not waste anything.
Do not get angry.
Do not complain.

My Three Vows:
Do not attempt the impossible.
Do not feel regret for the past.
Do not berate oneself.

My Three Joys:
Study.
Contemplation.
Haiku.

The one traditional Zen practice that Santōka was very
careful about was being satisfied with any amount and not
wasting anything. There are two well-known stories about
Santōka living by this precept told by Sumita Ōyama, Santō-
ka's close friend, editor, and biographer.

The first time Ōyama saw some of Santōka's poems in
Sōun he immediately wanted to meet him. However, Ōyama
knew that Santōka was continually on the road and difficult
to contact. When Ōyama heard that Santōka was staying at
Gochū-an, he wrote to him and arranged for a visit.

Soon after Ōyama arrived at Gochū-an, Santōka said to him:
"You must be hungry. Here, I've made some lunch for you."
He gave Ōyama a bowl of boiled rice and one hot pepper for
seasoning. Santōka told Ōyama to please begin eating. When

Ōyama suggested they eat together, Santōka said: "I have only one bowl."

After Ōyama finished his meal, Santōka took the bowl and ate the remainder of the rice and hot pepper. He then rinsed out the bowl in a bucket of water, took the water to wash off the floor and entranceway, and then went out to the garden with the remaining water. He called out: "Onions! Spinach! It's been a long time since you had some good food. Here's some special fertilizer for you."

Another time Ōyama had to spend the night at Gochū-an. There was naturally only one sleeping quilt, and Santōka insisted: "You are my guest. You use the quilt. I'll stay up." The quilt was little more than a ragged piece of cloth that would barely cover a child, let alone a full-grown man. As the winter wind blew in through the many holes in the walls and ceilings, Ōyama became colder and colder and was unable to sleep. Santōka put his priest's robe, his summer kimono, and several other pieces of cloth on top of Ōyama, but he was still cold. Finally, Santōka piled all his old magazines and even his little desk on top of his shivering friend. The next morning when Ōyama awoke, Santōka was still sitting in zazen.

Santōka was used to sharing anything he had. One night, as Santōka prepared for another dinnerless evening, a large dog came to his door carrying a big rice cake in its mouth. Santōka had no idea where the dog or the rice cake had come from. He took the rice cake, split it in two and gave half to the dog, who then ran off into the darkness. As soon as the dog was gone a little cat came up to Santōka and begged for some of the rice cake. Santōka split it again.

> *Aki no yo ya inu kara morattari neko ni ataetari*
> Autumn night—
> I received it from the dog
> And gave it to the cat.

These two *gathas* (Buddhist poems written in Chinese) describe Santōka's Zen:

Spring wind, autumn rain;
Flowers bloom, grass withers.
Self-nature is self-foolishness.
Walking on and on in the Buddha Land.

Intoxication has come as I lie on a stone pillow;
The sound of the valley stream never ceases.
Everything within the sakè, completely used up:
No self, no Buddha!

Sakè was Santōka's kōan. He said that "to comprehend the
true taste of sakè will give me satori." He attempted to com-
pletely efface himself through drinking, a practice not un-
known among certain types of Zen monks. Sitting for hours in
zazen in a monastery is difficult but perhaps not as difficult
as wandering through distant villages without money or food.
Casting off body and mind through sitting and solving kōans
is arduous training but so is truly using up everything within
the sakè: "When I drink sakè I do so with all my heart. I
throw myself recklessly into sakè drinking."

There is no point in romanticizing Santōka's alcoholism,
however. He himself struggled with this problem for many
years and never solved his greatest kōan. On several
occasions he was even arrested for public drunkenness and
vagrancy. He owed all of his friends money. Yet despite this
and all his other weaknesses, we still can find a profundity
and clarity in his poems that speak of a certain measure of
enlightenment. He had little self-pride, the last and greatest
obstacle to satori.

Santōka admitted that he could do only three things: walk,
drink sakè, and make haiku. Sakè and haiku were almost
identical:

Sakè for the body, haiku for the heart;
Sakè is the haiku of the body,
Haiku is the sakè of the heart.

Furthermore, haiku for Santōka was written Zen—spon-

24

taneous, sharp, clear, simple, direct. There must be nothing extra, no artifice, no straining. Haiku is like a *kiai,* the sudden resonant shout of a swordsman.* Since haiku flows from the depths of one's being, how can we be overly concerned with predetermined structure or theme? The most important element in Santōka's haiku is self-expression: "Haiku is not a shriek, a howl, a sigh, or a yawn; rather, it is the deep breath of life. In poetry we constantly examine life, occasionally shouting but never groaning. Sometimes tears fall, other times sweat flows; at all times we must savor each experience and move on without being obstructed by circumstances.

"Real haiku is the soul of poetry. Anything that is not actually present in one's heart is not haiku. The moon glows, flowers bloom, insects cry, water flows. There is no place we cannot find flowers or think of the moon. This is the essence of haiku. Go beyond the restrictions of your era, forget about purpose or meaning, separate yourself from historical limitations—there you'll find the essence of true art, religion, and science."

We can see from the above that while others maintained haiku to be literature or art, Santōka felt that haiku was life itself. He carved himself into each verse; creating haiku was his *samadhi,* a transcendent state of total absorption in his surroundings. "Sometimes clear, sometimes cloudy. Clear or cloudy I compose each verse in a state of body and mind cast off *(shinjindatsuraku).*"

Just before his death he wrote: "Every day I find myself in great difficulty. I don't know if I'll eat today or not. Death is approaching. The only thing I am able to do is to make poetry. Even if I don't eat or drink I cannot stop writing haiku. . . . For me, to live is to make haiku. Haiku is my life."

* "When composing a verse let there not be a hair's breadth separating your mind from what you write; composition of a poem must be done in an instant, like a woodcutter felling a huge tree or a swordsman leaping at a dangerous enemy."—Bashō

More than ten percent of Santōka's haiku
concern water—being drenched with it,
flowing with it, bathing in it, listening to
it, drinking it. Japan is a wet, humid country surrounded by
the sea and full of hot springs. Rain is the constant companion
of Japanese travelers. Many of Santōka's verses describe the
various possibilities of being soaked. Snowfall is rare in
southern Japan, where Santōka spent most of his life, but
winter rain is perhaps more chilling.

The water (in those days) was pure, good tasting, and abundant. Santōka's greatest joy was drinking cold water at the end
of a day's journey and warm sakè at night. For a time he
thought he even preferred water to sakè. His diet—water,
rice, sakè, *umeboshi* (pickled plum), *takuan* (pickled radish),
yudōfu—consisted of the simplest, most common, and least
expensive Japanese foods; yet when properly savored they are
the most delicious and nourishing foods there are.

Water was a symbol of his life and poetry—ever-flowing,
plain, simple, uncomplicated.

> *Hyōhyō to shite mizu o ajiwau*
> Aimlessly, buoyantly,
> Drifting here and there,
> Tasting the pure water.

Santōka's next favorite theme was weeds and wild grasses.
He often compared himself (and human beings in general) to
weeds. "Sprouting, growing, blooming, seeding, and withering, just as weeds, nothing more—that is good." Weeds are
everywhere, uncultivated, living with all their might, until
they wither away, die, and are reborn again the following
spring.

> *Shinde shimaeba zassō ame furu*
> When I die:
> Weeds, falling rain.

If weeds represent human existence, mountains are the

world of Buddha—vast, remote, sublime. Water and weeds are close to us, touchable, comprehensible; mountains appear mysterious, difficult to grasp.

> *Wake itte mo wake itte mo aoi yama*
> Going deeper
> And still deeper—
> The green mountains.

Although mountains seem to be impenetrably high and wide, Santōka threw himself into their depth. "Westerners like to conquer mountains; Orientals like to contemplate them. As for me, I like to taste the mountains."

FOOD FROM HEAVEN

"Today my path was wonderful. I wanted to shout out to the mountains, the sea, and the sky. The sound of the waves, the birds, the pure water—I'm grateful for everything. The sun shone brightly and the number of pilgrims increases daily. The memorials, the bridges, the shrines, and the cliffs were so beautiful. My rice was like food from heaven."

Santōka centered his life on the things directly in front of him. "Truth is seeing the new in the ordinary. Settle in this world. There are hidden treasures in the present moment." In his poetry he concerned himself with the simplest and most commonplace materials, for he understood that while "rice won't make you drunk, the essence of the rice will."

For Santōka any subject was suitable for poetry. Consequently, we find poems on almost every conceivable theme—nature, society, life and death, weeds, sex, the human body and its functions, the taste of water, sakè, and rice. Everything but history: "Do not be attached to the past or wait for the

future. Be grateful for each day, that is enough. I do not be-
lieve in a future world. I deny the past. I believe entirely in
the present. Employ your entire body and mind in the
eternal now.''

A NOTE ON THE   Perhaps the most attractive aspect of
TRANSLATIONS   Santōka's haiku is the utter simplicity of
                 his verses. Since he never uses literary or
historical allusions, or refined expressions, and keeps to
everyday language, the words of his haiku are easy to under-
stand. Naturally, the inner meaning of his poems is more
subtle, but it is never convoluted or involved. Hence most
of his haiku can be translated more or less directly into plain
conversational English.

Unfortunately, the beautiful rhythm, assonance, and ono-
matopoeia of many of the poems cannot be satisfactorily re-
produced in English. Therefore I have included romanizations
of the Japanese originals. Santōka's poems, and haiku in
general, are printed in one line with the reader supplying the
pauses. Following that custom, the Japanese originals appear
in one line without punctuation. Although Santōka's haiku
were written in an extremely free style with regard to the
5-7-5-syllable pattern, many seem to fall into a two-line pat-
tern, which I have reproduced, occasionally using three lines
where I felt it was warranted either by the Japanese original
or the English translation. At all times, my basic criterion for
translating has been, "How would Santōka say this in Eng-
lish?" My purpose has been to recreate Santōka's feelings in a
good free-style English haiku that can stand by itself as a valid
poem. Absolutely no effort has been made to analyze the poems
from a literary or any other standpoint.

The poems are not arranged in any order, although some
poems are grouped under a single theme. Haiku have been
taken both from Santōka's published collections and from
his journals.

ACKNOWLEDGMENTS Special thanks to Eidō Shimano Rōshi of Dai Bosatsu Zendō in New York for looking over an early version of the translations and offering many useful suggestions. I would also like to thank Robert Aitken Rōshi of the Diamond Sangha in Hawaii, who read the manuscript and discussed it with me, and Reb Anderson of the San Francisco Zen Center for arranging a talk on Santōka at the center which produced many interesting comments.

All the fine people at Weatherhill have my gratitude, especially Meredith Weatherby and Miriam Yamaguchi for their kind support and James T. Conte and Margaret Taylor for their excellent editorial guidance.

Joyce Stevens helped me with every phase of this book—conception, translating, typing, proofreading. I cannot thank her enough for her invaluable aid.

Santōka was photographed by Reireika Chikaki in Shimonoseki during a pilgrimage in 1933.

ZEN HAIKU

1

No path but this one—
I walk alone.

2

Begging: I accept
The blazing sun.

3

The pine branches hang down
Heavy with the chant:
Hail to the Bodhisattva of Compassion!

4

The wind in the pines
Morning and evening
Carries the sound of the temple bell.

1 *Kono michi shika nai hitori de aruku.*
2 *Enten o itadaite koiaruku.*
3 *Matsu wa mina eda tarete namu Kanzeon.* This was written in Santōka's first hermitage on the grounds of Mitori Kannon-dō, a temple dedicated to Kanzeon (Kannon) Bosatsu (Avalokiteshvara Bodhisattva).
4 *Matsu kaze ni ake kure no kane tsuite.* One of Santōka's duties at Mitori was to strike the small temple bell every day at 6 A.M. and 6 P.M.

5

The bucket full of rain:
It's enough for today.

6

Wet with morning dew,
I go in the direction I want.

7

Darkness,
  Wet with
The sound of the waves.

8

Alone I watch the moon
Sink behind the mountains.

5 *Ame o tamete baketsu ippai no kyō wa kototaru.*
6 *Asa tsuyu shittori ikitai hō e iku.*
7 *Nami no oto shigurete kurashi.*
8 *Ochikakaru tsuki o mite iru ni hitori.*
9 *Damatte kyō no waraji haku.* Straw sandals wear out quickly, and
   pilgrims generally carry several pairs with them. Santōka pon-

34

9

Silently, I put on
Today's straw sandals.

10

This straight road,
Full of loneliness.

11

Stretching out my feet;
Some daylight still remains.

12

Aimlessly,
I walk through the withered grass.

dered various kōans as he walked along, and on this particular
occasion he felt especially resolute as he put on a fresh pair of
sandals.

10 *Massugu na michi de samishii.*
11 *Nagedashite mada hi no aru ashi.*
12 *Ate mo naku fumiaruku kusa wa mina karetari.*

13

In the spring wind,
One small begging bowl.

14

My begging bowl
Accepts the fallen leaves.

15

Autumn heat—
My begging bowl
Is full of rice.

16

Hailstones, too,
Enter my begging bowl.

13 *Shumpū no hachi no ko hitotsu.* Begging bowls are often made of iron rather than wood so that they will be more durable. Santō-ka's was a large one holding one *shō* (1.8 liters) of sakè or water when not being used to carry rice or receive money. Generally, people in the towns give small coins, while those in the country give rice.

14 *Teppatsu chirikuru ha o uketa.*

15 *Aki atsui teppatsu de okome ga ippai.*

16 *Teppatsu no naka e mo arare.*

17

Spring—
  Walking with my begging bowl
Until the end.

18

  Going deeper
    And still deeper—
  The green mountains.

19

There is nothing else I can do;
I walk on and on.

20

  Slightly tipsy;
    The leaves fall
  One by one.

---

17 *Haru wa yuku hachi no ko motte doko made mo.*
18 *Wake itte mo wake itte mo aoi yama.* This was written in early
    summer in the mountains of Kumamoto Prefecture and is per-
    haps Santōka's best-known poem. Deeper and deeper into the
    human heart without being able to fathom its depth. . . .
19 *Dō shiyō mo nai watashi ga aruite iru.*
20 *Horohoro yōte ko no ha furu.* A *kasa* is a large woven straw hat
    worn by traveling monks to shield them from the sun and rain.

21

Not a cloud anywhere;
I take off my kasa.

22

Looking at the mountains;
All day no need
To put on my kasa.

23

The dragonflies
Perch on my kasa
As I walk along.

24

If the mountains are peaceful,
I remove my kasa.

21 *Mattaku kumo ga nai kasa o nugi.*
22 *Yama o miru kyō ichinichi wa kasa o kaburazu.*
23 *Kasa ni tombo o tomarasete aruku.*
24 *Yama shizukanareba kasa o nugu.*
25 *Kasa e pottori tsubaki datta.*

38

25

Oh! A big camellia
Bounced off my kasa.

26

Has my kasa
Also begun to leak?

27

From the back,
Walking away soaking wet?

28

These few ashes
Are all that remain
Of my diary?

---

26 *Kasa mo moridashita ka.*
27 *Ushiro sugata no shigurete yuku ka.* Santōka has said goodbye to his friends who have come to see him off. He turns and begins to walk away in the pouring rain wondering to himself: "What a sight I must be."
28 *Yakisutete nikki no hai no kore dake ka.*

The following three poems were written one night when Santōka was staying at a small inn. There wasn't enough space for all the travelers, and Santōka was put up in a tiny room with four other men.

29

Everyone else is sound asleep;
A bright moonlit night.

30

Just as I hoped:
Moonlight everywhere,
A night for insects.

31

Stretching out my feet,
They touch the man from Shikoku.

∽

32

No more houses to beg from;
The clouds cover the mountains.

29 *Minna nete shimatte yoi tsukiyo ka na.*
30 *Gekkō amaneku hoshii mama naru mushi no yoru da.*
31 *Nobashita ashi ni fureta tonari wa Shikoku no hito.*
32 *Mono kou ie mo naku nari yama ni wa kumo.*

33
I have no home;
Autumn deepens.

34
Daily torn and tattered,
Turning to shreds:
My robe for traveling.

35
The giant camphor tree, I,
And the dog
Are soaked through.

36
Separated by a screen:
Murmuring voices
Of men and women bathing.

33 *Ie o motanai aki ga fukō natta.*
34 *Kuchite mainichi hokorobiru tabi no hōe da.*
35 *Daishō mo watakushi mo inu mo shiguretsutsu.*
36 *Kabe o hedatete yu no naka no danjo sazamekiau.*

37

Flowing with the water
I walked down to the village.

38

The sunlight freely reflects off
My freshly shaven head.

39

Within life and death
Snow falls ceaselessly.

40

I walk in the wind's
Brightness and darkness.

37 *Mizu oto to issho ni sato e orite kita.*
38 *Soritate no atama ni zombun hi no hikari.*
39 *Shōji no naka no yuki furishikiru.*
40 *Kaze no meian o tadoru.*

41

At the foot of a mountain,
  Several graves stand together
In the warm sunlight.

42

  Daybreak: alone, I warm myself
  In the waters of the hot spring.

43

Swallows fly away—
  From today, more and more travels;
I tie on my straw sandals.

∾

Santōka once fell ill in a remote village. He recorded the following three haiku in his diary.

44

  I laid out my feverish body
  On the frozen earth.

41 *Yama suso atataka na hi ni narabu haka sukoshi ka na.*
42 *Akatsuki no yu ga watakushi hitori atatamete kuru.*
43 *Tsubame tobikau tabi kara tabi e waraji o haku.*
44 *Daichi hiebie to shite netsu no aru karada o makasu.*

45
Perhaps I'll die like this:
Lying on the cold earth.

46
Feverish—I stretch out
My body along the ground.

∾

47
(Spring planting:)
    Farmers and oxen
Both covered with sweat.

48
All together
    We pick the persimmons,
    We eat the persimmons.

45 *Kono mama shinde shimau ka mo shirenai tsuchi ni neru.*
46 *Netsu aru karada o naganaga to nobasu tsuchi.*
47 *Issho ni bisshori ase kaite ushi ga hito ga.*
48 *Minna issho ni kaki o mogitsutsu kaki o tabetsutsu.*

49

Nothing left to eat;
Today's sunrise.

50

If it shines, it bleats;
If it is cloudy, it bleats—
The single goat.

51

Now I stand here,
Where the ocean's blueness
Is without limit.

52

Warm fallen leaves;
I savor the rice's whiteness.

49 *Taberu mono mo naku natta kyō no asayake.*
50 *Tereba naite kumoreba naite yagi ippiki.*
51 *Ware ima koko ni umi no aosa no kagiri nashi.*
52 *Ochiba atatakaku kamishimeru gohan no hikari.*

53

Waking from a nap,
Either way I look: mountains.

54

Nice road
    Leading to a nice building.
It's a crematorium.

55

Wearing rags,
    In the coolness
I walk alone.

56

Well, which way should I go?
The wind blows.

53   *Hirune samete dochira o mite mo yama.*
54   *Yoi michi ga yoi tatemono e yakiba desu.*
55   *Boro kite suzushii hitori ga aruku.*
56   *Sate dochira e ikō kaze ga fuku.*

57

For once, both the futon and the night
Were long enough: deep sleep.

58

Sleeping on a soft futon,
I dream of my native village.

∾

After a long absence Santōka returned to his home town of
Sabare. He went to visit his younger married sister, whom he
hadn't seen in years. The children in the neighborhood tried
to chase him away, shouting: "Beggar, Beggar." His sister
was not glad to see him, and he was an unwelcome guest that
night. Very early the next morning she asked him to leave
before the neighbors saw him. She took him to the gate and
silently put fifty sen in his little bag.

59

I've come to a village
Where they use
The dialect of my home town.

---

57 *Futon nagaku yoru mo nagaku nesete itadaite.* A *futon* is a sleeping
quilt stored in a closet during the day and taken out at night.
58 *Futon fūwari furusato no yume.*
59 *Furusato no kotoba to natta machi ni kita.*

60

The long bridge—
  If I cross it
I'll be in my native village.

61

  Fireflies everywhere;
  I've returned to my native village.

62

Nothing remains
  Of the house I was born in—
Fireflies.

63

  Rain falls;
    I walk in my home town,
  Barefoot.

60 *Nagai hashi sore o watareba furusato no machi de.*
61 *Hōtaru koi koi furusato ni kita.*
62 *Umareta ie wa atokata mo nai hotaru.*
63 *Ame furu furusato wa hadashi de aruku.*
64 *Furusato wa atsukurushii haka dake wa nokotte iru.*
65 *Furusato no mizu o nomi mizu o abi.*

64

My home town—sweltering heat,
Nothing left but tombstones.

65

Water of my native village!
I drink it,
I wash with it.

66

I want to meet her but I can't—
My aunt's house is hidden in the green leaves.

67

I sit in the midst
Of my native dialect.

68

Incessant sound of waves—
My native place
Is more and more remote.

66   *Aitai ga aenai oba no ie ga aoba-gakure.*
67   *Furusato no kotoba no naka ni suwaru.*
68   *Nami oto no taezu shite furusato tōshi.*

69

Winter rain—
Everyone is drenched!

70

Pressing on and on,
    Until finally falling down;
The grass along the roadside.

71

After washing up
  I dry myself
On a nearby rock.

72

Oh! There is that friendly merchant
From China—Konnichi wa!

69   *Shigururu ya minna nurete iru.*
70   *Yuki yuki taoreru made no michi no kusa.*
71   *Arau to sono mama kawara no ishi ni hosu.* This was written at a
      roten-buro, an outdoor bath. Santōka was very fond of hot
      springs.
72   *Mata ōta Shina no ojisan konnichi wa.* Santōka often met the same
      people again and again in his travels. Since he stayed at the least
      expensive inns, he sometimes shared a room with poor mer-

73

In broken Japanese
   (The Korean)
Sells the candy.

74

Obediently blooming,
Becoming white flowers.

75

Eating my bentō—
It, too, is rain-soaked.

76

Oh! This louse
   I've caught
Is so warm!

chants from China and Korea. ''Konnichi wa'' is the usual day-time greeting in Japan.

73 *Obotsukanai Nihongo de ame ga yō ureru.*

74 *Sunao ni saite shiroi hana nari.*

75 *Tabete iru obentō mo shigurete.* A *bentō* is a small box lunch usually containing, in Santōka's time, rice and one *umeboshi* (pickled plum). These days they are more elaborate.

76 *Nanto atataka na shirami o toru.*

77

Potato gruel—
    Its warmth! Its good taste!
Autumn is here.

78

    The few flies that remain
    Seem to remember me.

79

(My favorite hot spring—)
    Bathing alone,
Sleeping alone.

80

    The small Buddha statue:
    Rained on for the sake of human beings.

77 *Imogayu no atsusa umasa mo aki to natta.*
78 *Ikinokoru hae ga watashi o oboete iru.*
79 *Hitori atatamatte hitori de neru.*
80 *Hito no tame ni shigurete Hotoke-sama.*

81
Sunset—the plowman's shadow
Grows deeper.

82
In the mountain all day,
The ants too are marching.

83
Aimlessly, buoyantly,
  Drifting here and there,
Tasting the pure water.

84
Baggage I cannot throw off,
So heavy front and back.

81 *Kurete nao tagayasu hito no kage koku.*
82 *Yama no ichinichi ari mo aruite iru.*
83 *Hyōhyō to shite mizu o ajiwau.*
84 *Sutekirenai nimotsu no omosa mae ushiro.*

85

Raising my voice above the wind:
Hail to the Bodhisattva of Compassion!

∾

The following verse was written by Seisensui when he visited
Santōka's hermitage, Gochū-an.

86

So this is what
    He calls his tea grove—
A single bush!

∾

87

In the early morning rain,
I sow the daikon seeds.

88

Winter rain—
    People have been so kind
My eyes fill with tears.

85   *Kaze no naka koe hariagete namu Kanzeon.*
86   *Kore de cha wa tariru to iu cha no ki.*

89

I slept soundly;
  I stretch out my body
In the hot water.

90

No water anywhere;
    Working in the dry rice field
The farmer sweats.

91

The thistles—
  Bright and fresh,
Just after the morning rain.

92

Peace for the heart:
Life in the mountains.

87 *Asayake ame furu daikon makō.*
88 *Shigururu ya hito no nasake ni namidagumu.*
89 *Netai dake neta karada yu ni nobasu.*
90 *Doko ni mo mizu ga nai kareta ase shite hataraku.*
91 *Azami azayaka na asa no ame agari.* The assonance and beauty of this poem in Japanese is impossible to reproduce in English.
92 *Kokoro shizuka ni yama no okifushi.*

93

I received them
  And they served my needs;
I put down my chopsticks.

94

  All day I said nothing—
  The sound of waves.

95

(In this neighborhood)
  Chanting the sutras
Cannot drown out the jazz music.

96

  Late at night:
  The harsh sound of gambling.

93 *Itadaite tarite hitori no hashi o oku.*
94 *Ichinichi mono iwazu nami oto.*
95 *Okyō todokanai jyazu no sōon.*
96 *Fukete bakuchi utsu koe.*
97 *Nageataerareta issen no hikari da.*
98 *Uma ga fuminijiru kusa wa hanazakari.*

97

The reflection of a one-sen coin
Thrown my way.

98

In the grass trampled by the horse:
Flowers in full bloom.

99

To the mountains,
    To the sky:
The *Heart Sutra*.

100

Each day we meet
Both demons and Buddhas.

99 *Yama e sora e Makahannya Haramitta Shingyō*. The one-page
Heart Sutra (Makahannya Haramitta Shingyō), shortest of all
Buddhist scriptures, is chanted from memory by Zen monks. Its
central theme is "form is emptiness, emptiness is form."
Emptiness (*Kū*) also means sky (*sora*). Santōka constantly chanted
this sutra.

100 *Ichinichi ni oni to Hotoke ni ai ni keri.*

101

The long black hair of the courtesans,
Disheveled by the salty breeze.

102

Coming and going
     In the twelfth month,
Nothing but strange faces.

103

(Together with an old friend)
     Eating dried cuttlefish
And talking of the past.

104

We've separated;
My backpack is heavy.

101 *Kurokami no nagasa o shiokaze ni makashi.*
102 *Shiwasu no yukiki no shiranai kao bakari. Shiwasu,* the twelfth
     month of the lunar calendar, is the busiest time of the year with
     everyone trying to settle their accounts and making prepara-
     tions for the New Year.
103 *Surume kamishimete wa mukashi o hanasu.*
104 *Wakarete kita nimotsu no omoi koto.*
105 *Gorori to kusa ni fundoshi kawaita.* A *fundoshi* is a loincloth worn
     by men.

105

Lying in the grass
I dry my fundoshi.

106

I offer incense
    To the Taneda mortuary tablet—
It is all that remains of my family.

107

I climb up the stone stairs
    Covered with winter rain:
Santa Maria.

108

Just as it is—
It rains, I get wet, I walk.

106   *Kore dake nokotte iru oihai o ogamu.* An *ihai* is a small memorial
      tablet with the family name on it, usually kept in a special altar
      at one's home or temple. Santōka carried his family's *ihai*
      with him since the land, ancestral home, and all the family's
      belongings were dissipated by Santoka's father.

107   *Fuyu ame no ishidan o noboru Santa Maria.* This was written at
      Santa Maria Church in Nagasaki, a city that is the site of many
      Christian churches and shrines.

108   *Furu mama nureru mama de aruku.*

109

All the paint
   Is worn off the Hotei statue,
But he continues to smile.

110

Urinating,
   I look down
On the sleeping village.

111

Completely drenched—
   This stone
Marks the way.

112

Cherry blossoms blooming,
   Cherry blossoms falling,
People dancing, dancing.

---

109   *Sukkari hagete Hotei wa waraitsuzukeru.* Potbellied statues of
      Hotei, a semi-mythical Chinese Zen monk who carries an enor-
      mous sack, are very common in Japan. Hotei is said to bring
      prosperity, and worshipers often rub his image for good luck.
110   *Nemuri fukai mura o mioroshi shito shite iru.*

113

My monk's robe
  Looks even more tattered,
Covered with grass seeds.

114

  I haven't met a soul;
  The road is bumpy.

115

Men, women,
  And their shadows
Dancing.

116

  The rain-soaked persimmon leaves
  Become even more beautiful.

---

111   *Shitodo ni nurete kore wa michishirube no ishi.*
112   *Sakura saite sakura chitte odoru odoru.*
113   *Hōe konna ni yaburete kusa no mi.*
114   *Dare ni mo awanai michi ga dekoboko.*
115   *Otoko onna to sono kage mo odoru.*
116   *Shigurete kaki no ha no iyoiyo utsukushiku.*

117
Spring cold—
I cross
From island to island.

118
Here again,
I shave off my white hair.

119
As they are,
The weeds
Sprout new buds.

120
In happiness
Or sadness,
Weeds grow and grow.

117 *Haru samui shima kara shima e watasareru.*
118 *Futatabi koko de shiraga o soru.*
119 *Aru ga mama zassō to shite me o fuku.*
120 *Ureshii koto mo kanashii koto mo kusa shigeru.*

121

Weeds that may die
    Any time—
Blooming and seeding.

122

    I sit in the withered beauty
    Of the wild grasses.

123

After all
    It's sad to be alone—
The withered grasses.

124

    After all
      It's good to be alone—
    The wild grasses.

---

121   *Itsu demo shineru kusa ga saitari minottari.*
122   *Kareyuku kusa no utsukushisa ni suwaru.*
123   *Yappari hitori wa samishii karegusa.*
124   *Yappari hitori ga yoroshii zassō.*

125

When I walk, weed seeds;
When I sit, weed seeds.

126

Dew and
    Fallen leaves,
Swept up together.

127

Walking in the wind
To receive some rice.

128

Why is such
A plaintive wind blowing?

125   *Arukeba kusa no mi suwareba kusa no mi.*
126   *Tsuyu mo ochiba mo minna hakiyoseru.*
127   *Kaze no naka kome morai ni iku.*
128   *Nande konna ni sabishii kaze fuku.*

129

A lonely night;
  Eating the leftover food,
And. . . .

130

  Completely dried up,
  They've become beans.

131

Tomorrow I will depart;
  Cherry blossoms
Falling, falling.

132

  In the evening loneliness,
  Again tilling the field.

129 *Samishii yoru no amarimono no taberu nado.*
130 *Sukkari karete mame to natte iru.*
131 *Asu wa kaerō sakura chiru chitte kuru.*
132 *Yūbe no samishisa wa mata hatake o utsu.*

133

In spring snow
Women are so beautiful.

134

One pot is enough;
I wash the rice.

135

The drifting clouds
And the temple's splendor
Reflect off the water.

136

Let's strike
The big temple bell!

133 *Haru no yuki furu onna wa makoto utsukushii.*
134 *Hitotsu areba kototaru nabe no kome o togu.*
135 *Kumo no yukiki mo eiga no ato no mizu hikaru.*
136 *Uraraka na kane o tsukō yo.*

137

Nonchalantly urinating
  By the road,
Soaking the young weeds.

138

Several ripe persimmons
  Left on the branches;
Gray clouds come and go.

139

I've made it this far;
I drink the pure water and go.

140

Thrusting my feet
  Into the rough sea—
My life as a traveler.

137 *Nombiri shito suru kusa no me darake.*
138 *Nokosareta futatsu mittsu ga jukushi to naru kumo no yukiki.*
139 *Koko made o koshi mizu nonde saru.*
140 *Araumi e ashi nagedashite tabi no atosaki.*

67

141

Squatting down on a sand dune—
    Today again,
Sado Island cannot be seen.

142

I enter the green forest
    Thinking of Ryōkan,
Who also passed this way.

143

My heart is empty;
The violent waves come and go.

144

In the thick grass,
    Puddles scattered
Among the temple ruins.

141 *Sakyū ni uzukumari kyō mo Sado wa mienai*. Sado is a very beautiful island in the Japan Sea off the coast of Niigata Prefecture in northern Honshu.

142 *Aoba wake yuku Ryōkan-sama mo ikashitaro*. Written on Mount Kugami near the site of Ryōkan's hermitage. Ryōkan (1758–1831) was an eccentric hermit-monk who spent much of his time playing with the local children, drinking sakè with the

145

At last! The moon and I
Arrive in Tokyo.

146

Since we parted,
Every day snow falls.

∽

The following poems, remarkable for their time and content,
are taken from a series written during the Japan-China war,
which broke out on July 7, 1937. No one in Japan was per-
mitted to oppose this conflict, and all poets were expected
to support the war effort in their works. Santōka, a beggar-
monk without a job, land, or a gun, nevertheless expressed his
true feeling in these poems.

147

I present my cool begging bowl as arms
At the six-o'clock siren.

farmers, and composing wonderful poems in a unique free-
style calligraphy.

143 *Kokoro munashiku aranami no yosete wa kaeshi.*
144 *Kusa no shigeru ya soseki tokorodokoro no tamari mizu.*
145 *Hotto tsuki ga aru Tōkyō ni kite iru.*
146 *Wakarete kara no mainichi yuki furu.*
147 *Suzushiku teppatsu sasagetsutsu gozen roku-ji no sairen.*

148

Marching together
  On the ground
They will never step on again.

149

Young men march away—
  The mountain greenness
Is at its peak.

150

Winter rain clouds—
  Thinking: Going to China
To be torn to pieces.

151

Eating this,
  The last Japanese meal,
They sweat.

148 *Futatabi wa fumumai tsuchi o fumishimete iku.*
149 *Minna dete iku yama wa aosa no iyoiyo aoku.*
150 *Shigurete kumo no chigireyuku Shina o omou.*
151 *Kore ga saigo no Nihon no gohan o tabete iru ase.*

152

The moon's brightness—
   Does it know
Where the bombing will be?

153

   Leaving hands and feet
      Behind in China,
   The soldiers return to Japan.

154

We move silently
   In the cold rain
Carrying the white boxes in front.

155

   Will the town
      Throw a festival
   For those brought back as bones?

152   *Tsuki no akarusa wa doko o bakugeki shite iru koto ka.*
153   *Ashi wa te wa Shina ni nokoshite futatabi Nihon ni.*
154   *Mokumoku to shite shigururu shiroi hako o mae ni.* The white boxes
       contain the ashes of the fallen soldiers.
155   *Machi wa omatsuri ohone to natte kaerareta ka.*

156
Soaking wet,
 Quietly returning
The remains of six hundred fifty.

157
Brave, yes;
 Sorrowful yes—
The white boxes.

158
Sweat trickles down
The white boxes.

159
The bones,
 Silently this time,
Returned across the ocean.

---

156 *Shiguretsutsu shizuka ni mo roppyaku gojū hashira.*
157 *Isamashiku mo kanashiku mo shiroi hako.*
158 *Poroporo shitataru ase ga mashiro na hako ni.*
159 *Ohone koe naku mizu no ue o yuku.*

160

The air-raid alarm
   Screaming, screaming;
Red persimmons.

～

161

Noon quiet—
   Cooking the eggplant,
Its burnt smell.

162

I sweep the garden
   After a long absence;
The flowers in the hedge are blooming.

163

Where the walls of my hut have crumbled
Vines and grass grow.

160 *Kūshū keihō ruirui to shite kaki akashi.*
161 *Hiru shizuka na yakinasu no yaketa nioi.*
162 *Hisashiburi ni haku kakine no hana ga saite iru.*
163 *Kabe ga kuzurete soko kara tsuru kusa.*

164

Mother! I am sharing
  The white noodles
Offered for your memorial day.

165

Pricks and pussies,
  Boiling together
In the overcrowded bath.

∾

These three verses were composed at Eihei-ji in Fukui Prefecture, the head temple of the Sōtō Zen school. Santōka spent six days training there. The day before he arrived he gave his robe and bowl to one of his friends and came dressed as a layman.

166

The butterfly—
  Floating, fluttering
Above the temple roof.

164 *Udon sonaete haha yo watakushi mo itadakimasuru.*
165 *Chimpoko mo ososo mo waite afureru yu.*
166 *Chōchō hirahira iraka o koeta.*

167

In the ceaseless sound
  Of the water
There is Buddha.

168

The Dharma Hall gates
  Are opened;
It becomes light.

∾

169

I slipped and fell—
The mountains are still.

170

Notes written before my trip,
Rewritten and put down.

167   *Mizuoto no taezu shite Mihotoke to ari.*
168   *Hattō ake hanatsu ake hanarete iru.*
169   *Subette koronde yama ga hissori.*
170   *Tabi no kakioki kakikaete oku.*

171

A single bird comes,
But does not sing.

172

It's enough;
I sweep up the fallen leaves.

173

Stretching out their branches—
The winter trees.

174

The frosty night—
Where am I going to sleep?

175

Using a stone for a pillow,
I drift toward the clouds.

171 *Ichiwa kite nakanai tori de aru.*
172 *Sore de yoroshii ochiba o haku.*
173 *Eda o sashinobete iru fuyuki.*
174 *Shimoyo no nedoko ga doko ka ni arō.*
175 *Ishi o makura ni kumo no yuku e o.*

176

Flowing down the mountain steepness:
The bright water.

177

The cawing crows,
The flying crows,
Have no place to settle down.

178

Throwing myself
Into the drenched mountains.

179

Making my way through the fallen leaves,
I have a good shit in the fields.

176 *Yama no kewashisa nagarekuru mizu no reirō.*
177 *Naite karasu no tonde karasu no ochitsuku tokoro ga nai.*
178 *Karada nagedashite shigururu yama.*
179 *Ochiba fumiwake hodo yoi noguso de.*

180

In the blazing sun:
  Railroad tracks,
Perfectly straight.

181

No inn to spend the night—
The moon leads the way.

182

It may be sunset,
  But still there is no inn;
Shrikes sing.

183

The dry, parched stones
Roll and roll.

180 *Enten no rēru massugu.*
181 *Tomete kurenai orikara no tsuki ga yukute ni.*
182 *Kurete mo yado ga nai mozudori ga naku.*
183 *Karete karekitte ishikoro gorogoro.*

184

A handful of rice,
  Received and eaten:
My daily travel.

185

  Behind, in front,
  Who can all these pilgrims be?

186

The days are short,
  Evening comes quickly;
My backpack is so heavy.

187

  Izu is warm now:
    I can sleep in the fields
    And listen to the sound of the waves.

184 *Ichiaku no kome o itadaki itadaite mainichi no tabi.*
185 *Ato ni nari saki ni nari ohenrosan no tarekare.*
186 *Tanjitsu kurekakaru oi no omosa yo.*
187 *Izu wa atatakaku nojuku ni yoroshii nami oto mo.*

188
Shining brightly
  In the sunshine :
My meal of boiled rice.

189
Birds in the rain—
They have nothing to eat.

190
Soaking wet—
  I can't read the letters
On the signpost.

191
Sitting by myself;
  The mosquitoes
  Won't leave me alone.

188   *Hinata mabushiku meshi bakari no meshi o.*
189   *Ame no torira wa taberu mono ga nai.*
190   *Shigurete sono ji ga yomenai michishirube.*
191   *Hitori de ka ni kuwarete iru.*

192

Today, still alive;
I stretch out my feet.

193

Some life remains;
I scratch my body.

194

The mountain stillness
Makes the rain still.

195

The sky at sunset—
A cup of sakè
Would taste so good!

196

Wearily I return (to my hut)
The moon fills the sky.

192 *Kyō made wa ikasareta ashi o nobasu.*
193 *Ikinokotta karada kaite iru.*
194 *Yama no shizukasa e shizukanaru ame.*
195 *Ippai yaritai yūyake-zora.*
196 *Tsukarete modoru tsuki bakari no ōzora.*

197

I walk along, begging;
The sound of water everywhere.

198

The evening shower clears up;
I go into the tomato field to eat.

199

That was my face
In the cold mirror.

200

Rocks and large cliffs,
Covered with crimson leaves.

201

The long night—
Made longer
By a dog's barking.

197 *Koiaruku mizu oto no doko made mo.*
198 *Yūdachi hareta tomato-batake ni dete taberu.*
199 *Sore wa watakushi no kao datta kagami tsumetaku.*
200 *Iwa ga ōki na iwa ga ichimen no tsuta kōyō.*
201 *Yoru no nagasa yodōshi inu ni hoerarete.*

202

Asleep or awake,
   The night is long—
The sound of the rapids.

203

    The beauty of the sunset
    Grieves not for old age.

204

Sitting alone,
   Silently, in the mosquito net,
Eating my rice.

205

    Working,
       And working harder;
    Still the pampas grass grows.

202 *Nete mo samete mo yoru ga nagai se no oto.*
203 *Yūyake no utsukushisa wa oi o nageku demo naku.*
204 *Mokumoku kaya no uchi hitori meshi kū.*
205 *Hataraite mo hataraite mo susukippo.*

206

More cutting,
  More digging,
Planting.

207

If only one plows the fields,
You'll soon hear a song.

208

Everyone has worked:
  The harvested rice fields
Extend on and on.

209

Alone on New Year's Day—
  There is mochi and sakè
And. . . .

---

206   *Karu yori horu yori maite iru.*
207   *Hitori tagayaseba utau nari.*
208   *Minna de hataraku karita hirobiro.*
209   *Hitori Shōgatsu no mochi mo sake mo ari soshite.* New Year's Day is
      the primary holiday of the year in Japan. The custom is for all
      the members of a family to gather together and enjoy eating

210

Settling down again;
  The distant mountains
Covered with snow.

211

  The fresh morning bath:
  Silently we wait in line.

212

So happy to be born,
  The baby opens
And closes his hands.

213

  Passing over the mountains,
  Again mountains, winter mountains.

mochi (rice cakes), drinking sakè, and playing traditional New
Year's games.

210 *Karada no mawari katazukete tōku yama nami no yuki.*
211 *Asayu no yoroshisa mokumoku to shite jumban o matsu.*
212 *Umarete ureshiku tanagokoro o nigittari hiraitari.*
213 *Koete yuku yama mata yama wa fuyu no yama.*

214

The cold sound
　Of a one-sen copper coin
Thrown my way.

215

Good news,
　Bad news;
Spring snow falls.

216

No road but this one;
Spring snow falls.

217

Beneath the River of Heaven
The drunkard dances all night.

214　*Nagete kudasatta issen dōka no samui oto datta.*
215　*Ureshii tayori mo kanashii tayori mo haru no yuki furu.*
216　*Kono michi shika nai haru no yuki furu.*
217　*Ama no kawa mayonaka no yoidore wa odoru.* The River of Heaven
　　is the Milky Way.

218

The deep, cool moon
Appears between the buildings.

219

Naked (in the bath house)—
The conversation
Grows more lively.

220

(New Year's Day—self-portrait)
Bundled up in rags,
A face full of New Year's greetings.

221

Moon! Mountains!
On this trip
I've fallen ill.

218 *Fukeru to suzushii tsuki ga biru no aida kara.*
219 *Hadaka de hanashi ga hazumimasu.*
220 *Boro kite kibukurete omedetai kao de.*
221 *Tsuki yo yama yo watashi wa tabi de yande iru.*

222
I've got a slight fever;
Hurrying in the wind.

223
Fallen leaves—
    Deep in the forest
I see a Buddha.

224
Winter sky—
    Distant dreams
Shattered and flown away.

225
Returning to my hut,
    One man's moon
Along the straight road.

222 *Sukoshi netsu ga aru kaze no naka o isogu.*
223 *Ochiba furu oku fukaku Mihotoke o miru.*
224 *Samuzora tōku yume ga chigirete tobu yō ni.*
225 *Kaeri wa hitori no tsuki ga aru ippon michi.*

226
Spring is here—
  Even my kitchen
Will be well stocked.

227
  At last it's cleared up;
  Today I too will do the wash.

228
At last the newlyweds' home is complete:
A new bucket.

229
  My endless journey—
  The smell of sweat.

226 *Haru ga kita watakushi no kuriya yutaka ni mo.*
227 *Yatto harete watakushi mo kyō wa osentaku.*
228 *Yatto shotai ga motete atarashii baketsu.*
229 *Hate mo nai tabi de ase kusai koto.*

230
Chanting the sutras,
    I receive the rice;
The shrikes sing.

231
Hurrying along the road,
I can't look back.

232
In the stillness
After the storm—flies.

233
I open the window
Full of spring.

234
Sunrise, sunset;
Nothing to eat.

230   *Okyō agete okome morōte mozu naite.*
231   *Furikaeranai michi o isogu.*
232   *Arashi no ato no shizukesa no hae de.*
233   *Mado akete mado ippai no haru.*
234   *Asayake yūyake taberu mono ga nai.*

235
Jumping:
One
Red frog.

236
Gradually I take on the vices
Of my dead father.

237
The mountain becomes dark,
I listen to its voice.

238
Summer heat
Soaks into
Every living thing.

235 *Tonde ippiki akagaeru.*
236 *Dandan nite kuru kuse no chichi wa mō inai.*
237 *Yama kurete yama no koe o kiku.*
238 *Mushiatsuku ikimono ga ikimono no naka ni.*

239
Sweat, gathered up
In my navel.

240
The nameless weed
Blooms all at once—purple.

241
Today's lunch:
Only water.

242
I can't give up sakè;
     The budding trees,
     The budding grasses.

243
A dragonfly on the rock;
Midday dreams.

239   *Heso ga ase tamete iru.*
240   *Na mo nai kusa no ichihayaku saite murasaki.*
241   *Kyō no ohiru wa mizu bakari.*
242   *Sake ga yamerarenai ki no me kusa no me.*
243   *Ishi ni tombo wa mahiru no yume miru.*

244

Spring—with an empty stomach
I walk along.

245

My new robe:
Full of sunlight and warmth.

246

Eggplants, cucumbers;
   Cucumbers, eggplants:
That's all I eat—the coolness.

247

High noon—in the deep grass
   The cry of a frog
Being swallowed by a snake.

244   *Haru wa utsuro na ibukuro o mochiaruku.*
245   *Atarashii hōe ippai no hi ga atatakai.*
246   *Nasu kyūri kyūri nasu bakari taberu suzushisa.*
247   *Hiru fukaku kusa fukaku hebi ni nomareru kaeru no koe.*

248
Picking the nameless flower,
I offer it to Buddha.

249
The cockroaches also
Have no food;
Did they eat my books?

250
My mind is clear;
I pick the frost-covered daikon.

251
I told a lie;
A lonely moon appears.

252
All the food completely eaten;
The weeds in full bloom.

248   *Tsunde kite na wa shiranu hana o Mihotoke ni.*
249   *Mushi mo taberu mono ga nai hon o tabeta ka.*
250   *Kokoro aratamete shimo no daikon o nuku.*
251   *Uso o itta sabishii tsuki no dete iru.*
252   *Taberu mono tabetsukushi zassō hanazakari.*

253

(After recovering)
　　I shave off my beard—
What deep wrinkles!

254

　　They could feel my hand;
　　The village flies escaped easily.

255

Scooping up the water,
　　Lifting it towards the moon,
Full of light.

256

　　Sunset full in my face;
　　　　After borrowing money
　　I return in the river wind.

253　*Tamatama hige soreba nanto fukai shiwa.*
254　*Utsute o kanjite machi no hae umaku nigeta.*
255　*Tsuki e kumiageru mizu no akarusa.*
256　*Irihi o matomo ni kane karite modoru kawakaze.*

Santōka sent this telegram to his teacher, Seisensui, on his fiftieth birthday.

257
The autumn sky—
   Far away
I share your joy.

∾

258
Autumn—one thing to pawn;
Taking it in, redeeming it.

259
From today
   I've no watch;
Evening rain.

260
Fully rested,
I open my eyes—spring.

257   *Akizora haruka ni ureshigaru. Santōka.*
258   *Shichigusa hitotsu dashitari iretari shite aki.*
259   *Kyō kara tokei o motanai yūbe ga shigureru.*
260   *Jūbun yasunda me ga aite haru.*

261

Dozing off,
  (My son) Ken visits me
In my dreams.

262

  Glad to be alive,
  I scoop up the water.

263

My hands, so thin
Even held together.

264

  I can't do anything;
    (My life of) contradictions,
  Blown by the wind.

261 *Utouto sureba Ken ga mimōte kureta yume.*
262 *Ikite iru koto ga ureshii mizu o kumu.*
263 *Konna ni yasete kuru te o awasete mo.*
264 *Dō suru koto mo dekinai mujun o kaze fuku.*

265

The brightness of the snow
Fills the house with calm.

266

I've something to eat
    And something to make me drunk;
Rain in the weeds.

267

Is there anything I lack?
The leaves fall.

268

Breaking the dead branches,
Thinking of nothing.

---

265 *Yuki no akarusa ga ie ippai no shizukesa.*
266 *Taberu mono wa atte you mono mo atte zassō no ame.*
267 *Nanika taranai mono ga aru ochiba suru.*
268 *Kare eda pokipoki omou koto naku.*
269 *Yatto yūbin ga kite sorekara jukushi no ochiru dake.* Since Santōka
    was almost continuously on the move, he would send his
    friends post cards informing them of his destination or the

269
At last
  The mail has come!
Soon the ripe persimmons will fall.

270
    Seeing off my friend,
    I return alone
    Trudging through the mud.

271
Today again no mail;
Dragonflies here and there.

272
    Destitute—melting snow
    Drips slowly from the roof.

sights he had seen, or containing several of his poems, and so on. Generally they would send back issues of poetry journals, news, and sometimes money that he would pick up at one of his stops.

270 *Hito o miokuri hitori de kaeru nukarumi.*
271 *Kyō mo yūbin ga konai tombo tobutobu.*
272 *Toboshii kurashi no yane no yuki tokete shitataru.*

273

In the sunlight
Jizō's face
Smiles brightly.

274

Rain falls silently;
I scoop up the water.

275

The green grass!
I return barefoot.

276

From the thicket
To the pot:
One bamboo shoot.

273　*Hizakari no O-Jizō-sama no kao ga nikoniko.* Stone statues of Jizō
　　　Bosatsu are often placed at crossroads or other places frequent-
　　　ed by travelers. Jizō (Ksitigarbha) is the patron of children and
　　　travelers and is usually shown standing, holding a pilgrim's
　　　staff in his right hand and a pearl in his left. His head is shaven,
　　　and he has a compassionate smile.

274　*Shōshō to furu mizu o kumu.*

277

No place to hide from the blazing sun;
The water flows by.

278

The warm water
   I brought back
Drops and spills.

279

The rain-filled bucket
Brimming with beautiful water.

280

There is still something to eat:
The cool water.

275 *Kusa no aosa yo hadashi de modoru.*
276 *Yabu kara nabe e takenoko ippon.*
277 *Enten kakusu tokoro naku mizu no nagarekuru.*
278 *Morōte modoru atataka na mizu no koboruru o.*
279 *Ame o ukete oke ippai no utsukushii mizu.*
280 *Taberu mono ga nakereba nai de suzushii mizu.*

281

Sweeping, falling,
   Sweeping, falling:
Late autumn.

282

The leaves fall;
   From now on,
Water will taste even better.

283

From the shadow
   Of the rocks
Water wells up.

284

No sakè;
   I stare at the moon.

281   *Haku hodo ni chiru hodo ni aki fukaku.*
282   *Ochiba suru kore kara mizu ga umaku naru.*
283   *Iwa kage masashiku mizu ga waite iru.*
284   *Sake wa nai tsuki shimijimi mite ori.*

285

Such delicious water
Overflows from the spring.

286

Drunk, I slept
With the crickets.

287

What a splendid inn!
Mountains in both directions
And a sakè shop in front.

288

Holding a tomato as an offering,
I place it before Buddha,
Before my mother and father.

285 *Konna ni umai mizu ga afurete iru.*
286 *Yōte kōrogi to nete ita yo.*
287 *Yoi yado de dochira mo yama de mae wa sakaya de.*
288 *Tomato o tanagokoro ni Mihotoke no mae ni chichi haha no mae ni.*

289

Tombstones in a row—
Penetrating silence.

290

The willow leaves are falling;
From there I'll begin begging.

291

From the child's full hands
I receive each grain of rice,
One by one.

292

Walking in the freezing wind,
Bitterly reproaching myself.

289 *Narande ohaka no shimijimi shizuka.*
290 *Yanagi chiru soko kara koihajimeru.*
291 *Otete koboreru sono hitotsubu hitotsubu o itadaku.*
292 *Kaze no naka onore o semetsutsu aruku.* Once Santōka accidentally wandered into a red-light district on one of his begging trips and unexpectedly received money from several prostitutes. He used that money to buy the services of one of the girls in a nearby quarter.

293

The sky above,
The bentō in my hands,
Sunlight all around,
The rice's whiteness.

294

Walking on and on
Among the endless
Blooming higan flowers.

295

Thirsty for a drink of water—
The sound of a waterfall.

296

Sometimes I stop begging
And gaze at the mountains.

293 *Sora takaku bentō itadaku hikari amaneku gohan shiroku.*
294 *Arukitsuzukeru higanbana sakitsuzukeru.* *Higan* flowers (cluster amaryllis, *Lycoris radiata*) bloom during the autumn equinox, when Buddhist services are held for the dead.
295 *Nomitai mizu ga oto tatete ita.*
296 *Aruiwa kou koto o yame yama o mite iru.*

297

Far, far away,
　A bird crosses over
The snow-covered mountains.

298

　　The distant snow-covered mountains—
　　Completely cut off from the world of men.

299

People gather around the dead man;
No clouds in the sky.

300

　　　The warmth of the food
　　　Passes from hand to hand.

301

Already the wet baggage
Feels heavy—another pilgrimage.

297　*Tōku tōku tori wataru yamayama no yuki.* In Japan one's soul is said
　　　to ascend to heaven in the form of a bird.
298　*Enzan no yuki mo wakarete shimatta hito mo.*

302

The hermit is away;
  In his absence
I strike his mokugyō.

303

Wet with evening dew,
I slept.

304

If I sell my rags
  And buy some sakè
Will there still be loneliness?

305

The military parade grounds
  Also have the day off—
The skylarks twitter.

299 *Shibito torimaku hitobito ni kumo mo naki sora ya.*
300 *Tabemono atatakaku te kara te e.*
301 *Nurete nimotsu no sara ni omotaku tabi.*
302 *Anshu wa orusu no mokugyo o tataku.* A *mokugyo* is a wooden
    drum used to accompany sutra chanting.
303 *Yotsuyu shittori nemutte ita.*
304 *Boro utte sake kōte samishiku mo aru ka.*
305 *Rempei mo kyō wa oyasumi no hibari saezuru.*

306

(My beard's theme song:)
    An uneven life,
Standing and falling.

307

In the heat of the day
    Crying or laughing—
Only one.

308

I've rice,
    Books,
And tobacco.

309

Only wishing to walk,
    I walk with my full sack—
The evening moon.

306   *Kurashi chiguhagu na hige o tatetari otoshitari.*
307   *Hizakari naite mo warōte mo hitori.*
308   *Gohan ga atte hon ga atte soshite tabako mo atte.*
309   *Arukitai dake aruite zudabukuro fukureta yūzuki.*

310

Twilight—the sound
  Of the sad letter dropping
Into the postbox.

311

Using a stone for a pillow,
Truly sleeping: this beggar.

312

All day I said nothing;
  Unable to sleep—
The moonlit night.

313

Frying fish,
  Sometimes frying your hand—
Life alone.

---

310 *Kanashii tegami o posuto ni otosu oto no yūyami.*
311 *Ishi o makura ni shite shinjitsu nete iru kojiki.*
312 *Ichinichi mono iwazu nemurenai tsukiyo to naru.*
313 *Sakana yaku tote te o yaku koto mo hitori-gurashi no.*

314

In the sunlight on my desk
I write a long, long letter.

315

Without any destination
I walk between the tombstones.

316

The deep, clear blue water
    Shines brightly—
My sad shadow.

317

In the boiling sun
    (The construction workers)
Heat lead.

314 *Hinata e tsukue o nagai nagai tegami o kaku.*
315 *Nantonaku aruite haka to haka to no aida.*
316 *Massao sumu mizu urara teru waga kage kanashii.*
317 *Enten no machi no mannaka namari ni yu.*

318

From the mountains:
  White wildflowers
On the desk.

319

  In the space between the buildings—
  Look at the mountain's greenness!

320

Cold
  Clouds
Hurrying.

321

  The reflection in the water:
  It's a traveler.

318 *Yama kara shiroi hana o tsukue ni.*
319 *Biru to biru no sukima kara miete yama no aosa yo.*
320 *Samui kumo ga isogu.*
321 *Mizu ni kage aru tabibito de aru.*

111

322

A beautiful spring has arrived
Next to the cemetery.

323

Beneath the midsummer sky
At midday
A baby cries.

324

The clear, cold, starry sky—
The mountain ascetics beat their drums.

325

Winter has set in—
Pieces of wood, pieces of bamboo.

322 *Bochi o tonari ni yoi haru ga kita.*
323 *Manatsu mahiru no sora no shita nite akago naku.*
324 *Hoshizora saete kuru kangyō no taiko uchidashita. Kangyō* is a
thirty-day period in the coldest part of winter set aside for
special austerities by certain religious groups, especially
yamabushi, priests who combine both Shinto and Buddhist eso-
teric practices. At night they walk through the mountains and

326

The moon rises—
I'm not waiting for anything.

327

The rain from that cloud
Made me wet.

328

It's fall—
I sit in the wild grasses.

329

Travelers,
Travelers,
Coming together, parting.

nearby towns virtually naked, beating large drums and chant-
ing the name of Buddha.

325   *Fuyu ga kite iru kigire takegire.*
326   *Tsuki ga nobotte nani o matsu demo naku.*
327   *Ano kumo ga otoshita ame ni nurete iru.*
328   *Aki to natta zassō ni suwaru.*
329   *Tabibito tabibito to wakare yuku.*

330

A stomach full of water;
I sleep soundly.

331

(Meeting an old friend:)
Two old faces—
Silence.

332

I sow the seeds
In the morning sunlight
Before departing on a journey.

333

Cherry blossoms
In full bloom—
The prison.

330 *Hara ippai mizu nonde kite neru.*
331 *Toshitotta kao to kao to de damatte iru.*
332 *Asa no hikari e maite oite tabidatsu.*
333 *Sakura mankai ni shite keimusho.*

334

Snow falls—in my hut
I kindle a fire for one.

335

Snow falls
   On the snowfall
Silently.

336

Even snow cannot be good snow;
The smoke from the factories.

337

(To a friend)
   Tomorrow I'll come.
Cooking wild vegetables
For your visit.

334 *Gochū yuki furu hitori toshite hi o taku.*
335 *Yuki e yuki furu shizukesa ni oru.*
336 *Yuki mo yoi yuki ni naranai kōjō chitai no kemuri.*
337 *Asu wa kuru to iu ame no fuki o nite oku.*

338

Everyone is telling lies;
Spring has been chased away.

339

I'll never be crossing
This bridge again;
The wind blows long and hard.

340

Truly a mountainous country!
Only mountains, more mountains,
And the bright moon.

341

(Returning home)
In the deep stillness—
The dust on the desk.

338   *Minna uso ni shite haru wa nigete shimatta.*
339   *Futatabi wa wataranai hashi no nagai nagai kaze.*
340   *Makoto yamaguni no yama bakari naru tsuki no.*
341   *Shimijimi shizuka na tsukue no chiri.*

342

The cut, without healing,
    Becomes cold and chapped.
Winter confinement.

343

    The starving cat cries;
    I have nothing to give him.

344

Thinking of nothing,
    I walk among
A forest of withered trees.

345

    (Meeting again,)
    We clasp each other's
    Chapped hands.

342   *Kizu ga sono mama akagire to nari fuyu komoru.*
343   *Uete naki yoru neko ni ataeru mono ga nai.*
344   *Omou koto naku kareki o hiroi arukitsutsu.*
345   *Nigirishimeru te ni te no akagire.*

346

The sound of the waves—
   Now distant, now close:
How much of my life remains?

347

I purify myself
   In the blue water
Rushing over the rocks.

348

The moonlight
   Pierces
My empty stomach.

349

I lack the barest essentials;
The water flows.

346   *Nami oto tōku nari chikaku nari yomei ikubuku zo.*
347   *Iwabashiru mizu ga tataeshi aosa misogi suru. Misogi* is an ascetic
      practice to purify one's body and mind. Prayers or sutras are
      recited while the devotee stands under a waterfall or in a river,
      usually during the coldest time of the year.
348   *Tsuki no hikari no sukihara fukaku shimitōru nari.*

350

Searching for what?
I walk in the wind.

351

Slapping at the flies,
    Slapping at the mosquitoes,
Slapping at myself.

352

Even the sound of the raindrops
Has grown older.

353

It can't be helped;
    My old robe
Is rotting away.

349   *Toboshii kurashi no mizu no nagaruru.*
350   *Nani o motomeru kaze no naka yuku.*
351   *Hae o uchi ka o uchi ware o utsu.*
352   *Amadare no oto mo toshitotta.*
353   *Mamayo hōe wa aka de kuchita.*

354

Hidden away in
A broken-down hut,
My broken-down life.

355

No one has come;
The cayenne peppers
Have turned bright red.

356

The breeze from the mountains
In the wind bell
Makes me want to live.

357

Slowly, slowly
Falling into ruin—
My final autumn.

354 *Kuzureru ie no hisoka ni kuzureru higurashi.*
355 *Dare mo konai tōgarashi akō naru.*
356 *Yama kara kaze ga fūrin e ikite itai to omou.*
357 *Horohoro horobiyuku watakushi no aki.*
358 *Moto no kojiki ni natte taoru ga ichimai.* Near the end of his life
Santōka was ashamed of his behavior and told his friends he

358

I've become a real beggar;
One towel.

359

Today again, soaking wet,
I walk on an unknown road.

360

Red urine—
How long will I be able
To continue this journey?

361

I can't stop coughing—
There is no one to slap my back.

wanted to stop pretending to be a Zen priest. He gave away his
bowl and priest's robe; all he had left was a tattered kimono
and one towel to wrap around his waist.

359 *Kyō mo nurete shiranai michi o yuku.*
360 *Akai shito shite itsu made tabi o tsuzukeru koto ka.*
361 *Seki ga yamanai senaka o tataku te ga nai.*

362

No money, no things,
  No teeth—
All alone.

363

My heart is weary—
  The mountains, the sea
Are too beautiful.

364

When will I die?
I plant the seedlings.

365

Mountains I'll never see again
Fade in the distance.

362 *Zeni ga nai mono ga nai ha ga nai hitori.*
363 *Kokoro tsukarete yama ga umi ga utsukushisugiru.*
364 *Itsu shinuru ki no mi wa maite oku.*
365 *Mata miru koto mo nai yama ga tōzakaru.*

366

Nothing left but to die;
Mountains lost in mist.

367

(Sickness)
　　　Death is before me;
The cool breeze.

368

Settling down to die—
Withered grasses.

369

　　　Settling down to die—
Sprouting grasses.

370

I cling to death;
The pepper is bright red.

366 *Shinu yori hoka nai yama ga kasunde iru.*
367 *Shi o mae ni suzushii kaze.*
368 *Ochitsuite shinesō na kusa karuru.*
369 *Ochitsuite shinesō na kusa moyuru.*
370 *Shi o hishito tōgarashi makka na.*

371

The quietness of death:
A clear sky, leafless trees.

372

When I die:
Weeds, falling rain.

371 *Shi no shizukesa wa harete ha no nai ki.*
372 *Shinde shimaeba zassō ame furu.*

BIBLIOGRAPHICAL NOTE

The complete works of Santōka (*Teihon Taneda Santōka Zenshū*) in seven volumes edited by Sumita Ōyama have been published by Shun'yōdō (Tokyo 1972). The first volume contains the poems published during Santōka's lifetime (approximately 800), while his travel journals, diaries, and essays comprise the remaining six volumes. Ōyama has published a separate collection, *Teihon Taneda Santōka Kushū* (Yayoi Shobō, Tokyo 1971) that includes the 800 poems together with some selected haiku taken from the journals. Kōbunsha, also of Tokyo, has put out a six-volume series on Santōka: three volumes of journals (*Ano Yama Koete, Kono Michi o Yuku, Gu o Mamoru*), one collection of poems (*Sōmokutō*), a biography by Toshi Ueda (*Haijin Santōka*), and Santōka's sayings (*Santōka o Kataru*) edited by Seisensui Ogiwara.

OTHER VALUABLE STUDIES OF SANTŌKA,
IN JAPANESE, INCLUDE:

Kaneko, Tōta. *Taneda Santōka: Hyōhaku no Haijin.* Tokyo: Kōdansha Gendai Shinsho, 1974.

Kino, Kazuyoshi. *Henreki no Honami no Sekai.* Tokyo: NHK Books, 1977.

Koyama, Eiga. *Santōka no Hyōhaku.* Tokyo: Kaibisha, 1973.

Murakami, Mamoru. *Santōka, Kyōgai to Haiku.* Tokyo: Shōwa Shuppan, 1978. This book contains a comprehensive bibliography of Santōka's works and a complete list of all books and articles about him.

Onozawa, Mamoru. *Inochi Hitori: Santōka Kanshō.* Tokyo: Sōgensha, 1973.

Ōyama, Sumita. *Haijin Santōka no Shōgai.* Tokyo: Yayoi Shobō, 1971.

In English see:

Abrams, James. "Hail in the Begging Bowl: the Odyssey and Poetry of Santōka," *Monumenta Nipponica*, vol. 3 (Autumn, 1977).

Blyth, R. H. *A History of Haiku*. Vol. 2. Tokyo: Hokuseidō, 1964.

The "weathermark" identifies this book as a production of John Weatherhill, Inc., publishers of fine books on Asia and the Pacific. Book design and typography: Meredith Weatherby and Miriam F. Yamaguchi. Composition of the text: Samhwa Printing Company, Seoul. Printing of the text: Toyo Printing Company, Tokyo. Binding: Makoto Binderies, Tokyo. The typeface used is Monotype Perpetua.